D1214124

PRAISE FROM CAT EXPERTS

"This is an **absolutely delightful book** intended for children, but actually one that is informative for adults as well, it reinforces the importance of considering various factors when selecting a cat as a pet. The two cousins are exchanging thoughts about their lifestyles and priorities. They each have a vision of their 'ideal cat.' Though every cat is an individual, the book expresses the value of predictable personality traits and other characteristics of various pedigreed cat breeds. It is a charming story of the two children each going through the process of finding a cat who best fits their own preferences. The **playful illustrations compliment the humorous and educational quality of the book**."
— Joan Miller, Cahir, CFA Outreach and Education, Cat Fancier's Association

This is **quite simply as informative a cat book as any text out there**. Each selected breed pinpoints the single most important trait to know about it before choosing a cat 'purrfect' for you. Although written from a child's perspective, it makes clear sense to readers of all ages. As a cat lover and Maine Coon Cat breeder and enthusiast, I was thrilled with the spot on description and story of this beloved breed.
— Alexis Mitchell, Syracoon/Furensics, Maine Coon Cat Breed Council Secretary, Maine Coon Cat breeders of CFA

"*I Want a Cat: An Opinion Essay*" by Darcy Pattison is a **delightful** book. Being both a teacher who works with dyslexic students, and a breeder of pedigreed cats, I would **highly recommend this book to young writers**. The importance of good writing skills are stressed by using a creative and entertaining story. It would be a book that I would recommend to my colleagues who teach younger students. I also like that the book introduces several breeds of pedigreed cats, as well as responsible pet ownership in using criteria to determine what breed of cat is best for suited for their families. It is refreshing to see responsible pet ownership presented to younger children. "
— Julie Keyer, Faculty, The Lewis School of Princeton, CFA Breed Council Secretary, Oriental Cats

Other Mims House Books:
MimsHouse.com

Wisdom, the Midway Albatross: Surviving the Japanese Tsunami and other Disasters for Over 60 Years. Starred PW review, 2014-15 Sakura Medal Reading List – Children's book award from the English speaking schools in Japan.

Abayomi, the Brazilian Puma: The True Story of an Orphaned Cub
 (nonfiction picture book)
 2015 Science Teacher's Association Outstanding Science Trade Book
Saucy and Bubba: A Hansel and Gretel Tale *(novel)*
The Girl, the Gypsy and the Gargoyle *(novel)*
Vagabonds: An American Fantasy *(novel)*
The Aliens, Inc. Chapter Book Series
 Kell, the Alien, Book 1
 Kell and the Horse Apple Parade, Book 2
 Kell and the Giants, Book 3
 Kell and the Detectives, Book 4 *(March 2015)*

Read Other Books in The Read and Write Series

 I Want a Dog: My Opinion Essay
 My Crazy Dog: My Narrative Essay *(Fall 2015)*

MimsHouse.com/newsletter
Get a free eBook - on us!

By Darcy Pattison

Illustrations by
Ewa O'Neill

I Want a Cat:
My Opinion Essay

I Want a Cat: My Opinion Essay

Paperback 978-1-62944-033-0
Hardcover 978-1-62944-032-3
eBook 978-1-62944-034-7

Library of Congress Control Number:
2014913874

Mims House
1309 Broadway
Little Rock, AR 72202
USA

Acknowledgments:
Thanks to Joan Miller, Cat Fancier's
Association for her help
in sorting out the
cat breeds.

My cousin, Dennis, and I got dogs last year. Now, we want cats. We have been emailing about what kind of cat to get.

And now, at school, I have to write an essay about the best cat breed for our family.

My teacher, Mr. Eagle, says, "Mellie, you have to have criteria."

Of course, I have good reasons for the kind of cat I want.

Birman

Cornish
Rex

MY CRITERIA:
Active or Lazy?
I want a cat that pounces.
Dennis wants a lazy cat,
like his lazy dog, Clark Kent.

Siberian

Playful or not?
My cat should love
to play with string
or paper.

Devon
Rex

Dennis says that's OK, as long as
the cat doesn't scratch the new
baby when it comes.

Needs lots of attention? While I am at school, Grandma takes care of our Maltese dog, Lois Lane. Now, Lois Lane thinks she's Grandma's pet. This time, the cat will sleep in my room and love me the most.

Siamese

Dennis won't spend much time with his cat because he plays baseball and walks Clark Kent.

American Shorthair

Needs for affection?
I want a cat
that sits in
my lap.

Burmese

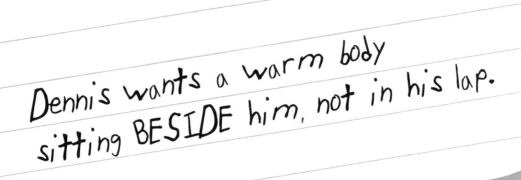

Dennis wants a warm body sitting BESIDE him, not in his lap.

Norwegian Forest

Lots of meowing
or quiet?

Grandma takes
afternoon naps,
so our pets must
be quiet.
That new baby at
Dennis's house
will need a quiet
cat, too.

Egyptian
Mau

Waaaa
Waaaa
Waaaaaaa

Ragdoll

Sphynx

Hard or easy to handle?

We both want cats that won't fuss when you pick them up.

Russian
Blue

Intelligent?
Smart cats love
the person who
takes care
of them.
That's me!

Oriental

Dennis says
he wants a
smart one, too,
but one who
Knows enough
not to get into
trouble.

Independent?

I do dance and piano classes, and Grandma just taught me to play chess. So, I can't take care of a cat all the time.

British
Shorthair

Dennis says his cat needs to take care of itself all day. He just wants the cat to sleep on his bed. (Psst! His mom caught Clark Kent on Dennis's bed, and she was MAD.)

Persian

Lots of grooming?
I like brushing out a cat. I still
brush out Lois Lane's long hair.

Dennis says, "NO! NO! NO!"

Tonkinese

Maine Coon

Other pets?
We both have dogs, so
our cats have to get
along.

Abyssinian

I Want a Cat

I want a cat. I thought hard about what kind of cat I wanted. First, I want a giant cat, maybe as big as Lois Lane, our Maltese dog. I don't want a tiny cat that will get lost in the house. A big cat might be heavy, but I am strong and will be able to carry it.

Also, I don't care if it likes strangers, as long as it's nice to everyone in our family. I like a cat that purrs, sits still, and has thick fur. I like to scratch behind a cat's ears.

Sometimes after dance class, I'm tired. Therefore, I just want to flop onto the floor. I want to dangle a piece of string and let my cat chase it. When we're both tired

A Excellent!

from dancing around, I want the cat to sit quietly on my lap because I will play chess with Grandma.

Since I looked at cat breeds and thought about my criteria, I made a decision. The best cat for our family is a Maine Coon Cat. It will be nice and will keep surprising me. It will play with simple toys and sleep on my bed at night. I will love my purring alarm clock.

I got an A on my essay! And when Mom and Dad read my amazing essay, I got —

—a Maine Coon Cat
named Ken!

Dennis got
a Russian Blue cat named
Barbie. (Guess who got to name
them this time?)

Here's a surprise. Ken likes to watch our fish pond. Most cats don't like water, but I think he wants to jump in and swim. He even likes to dunk his food in his water bowl.

Now when I get home, I go to the kitchen and get a glass of milk. Ken appears like magic and rubs against my legs. We sit on the kitchen floor and have a quiet talk. Then we go and talk to Grandma about her day.

And, here's one more thing. Dennis, has a new sister! We will go next week to see my new cousin, Ruth – Wah! Clark Kent will get to see Lois Lane again – Woof! And Ken and Barbie will meet for the first time –
Meow!

Writing with Kids about Cats

How to Choose a Cat
- Shared or Individual Research Project

For a shared or individual research project, AnimalPlanet.com offers an interactive Cat Breed Selector tool (http://www.animalplanet.com/breedselector/catselectorindex. do), which uses criteria to narrow the choices to a few appropriate breeds. A how-to essay can concentrate on the importance of using criteria to select a cat. This story includes nine criteria: energy level, play needs, need for attention, affectionate, vocalizations, ease of handling, intelligence, independence, grooming needs, and getting along with other pets. Other criteria might include allergies, weather related issues, family traditions, price, male or female, availability in your area, and specific needs such as a cat to show. Students can choose the most important criteria for their family and write about how to choose the right dog for them.

I Want a Cat - Opinion Essay

This book is a model text for writing about what kind of cat is best for a family. Students could write Dennis's essay about choosing the Russian Blue. To write about their own family, students should do prewriting about their criteria or reasons for choosing a certain cat breed.

Cat Breeds - Informative Essay

Use this book as prewriting to help students narrow their focus to just one or two breeds of cat that interest them. From there, students can research dog breeds at The Cat Fanciers' Association (http://www.cfainc.org/) or in a variety of informational books.

Imagined or Real Narrative

Students can use this book as an example for a real or imagined narrative about a girl or boy getting a cat or other pet.

10 Popular Cat Breeds*

British Shorthair

Siamese

Ragdoll

Abyssinian

Exotic

Sphynx

American Shorthair

Maine Coon

Devon Rex

Persian

* Source: http://www.cfa.org/News/PressReleases/PressReleaseTop10Breeds.aspx